Reflections
of Life

Reflections of Life

Richard de Roza

PARTRIDGE

A Penguin Random House Company

Library of Congress Control Number: 2015936942
ISBN: Softcover   978-1-4828-3090-3
                   eBook   978-1-4828-3091-0

To order additional copies of this book, contact
Toll Free 800 101 2657 (Singapore)
Toll Free 1 800 81 7340 (Malaysia)
orders.singapore@partridgepublishing.com

www.partridgepublishing.com/singapore

Introduction

Dear Reader

My main purpose of writing this book on Reflections of Life is to give some inspiration to others.

I am always inspired when reading books from different authors, fiction and non-fiction stories.

It has helped so much in life to be patient, to be encouraged and motivated in what I am doing either in work or in family life.

The chapters that you are about to explore are real life stories and experience from someone who has gone through ups and downs in life. It is about a family going through life like a roller-coaster.

Any resemblance to the names in this book is purely coincidental.

So I hope you will enjoy reading as much as I have enjoyed penning this book.

Thank you

Prologue

Dear Reader

It is through inspiration that instils me to write this book on Reflections of Life.

What really is Reflections of Life? It is simply a life for all of us to reflect upon.

It is the life that we are living and then we will die one day.

The life to all of us is a life that we should go on living, be satisfied with what we have.

The more we have, the more we want and then what happens after that?

Reflections of Life are not meant to be this way of living.

Reflections of Life are meant for us to live as we deem fit to go on living a life that we can appreciate what is around us, what can make us be satisfied and live a fulfilling life.

So dear reader, I hope that this book can give you inspiration as much as it has given me to reflect on the importance of our lives.

We are created to live this life as much as to fulfil and to live a life to the fullest.

This book is not meant just to read like a novel, but to allow you to ponder, reflect and be inspired. After reading it, do not just put it aside but re-read it another time.

This book is meant to be with you as long as you are able to grasp the contents in it to be inspired and re-live a life so fulfilling that you will not be down and trouble. This book is meant to enlighten you dear reader.

Finally, whenever you feel down, troubled, having problems in whatever incidence occur, pick up this book and read those chapters that will make your heart be unburden and light.

There are number of chapters in this Reflections of Life.

Life-loving is the first chapter and Life-giving is the second chapter.

Others in line are – Life- Radiance, Life-Upheaval, Life-fulfilment, Life-Journey, Life-Reasoning, Life-Searching, Life-Controlling.

Life-Loving

"Life isn't about finding yourself. Life is about creating yourself."

-George Bernard Shaw

"Whether humanity will consciously follow the law of love, I do not know. But that need not disturb me. The law will work just as the law of gravitation works whether we accept it or not."
Mahatma Ghandi (1869-1948) Indian Political Leader

What Albert Einstein quoted about life, is this – life is like riding a bicycle. To keep your balance you must keep moving. Isn't this really true for all of us to live life to be well balanced? So what life really is?

It has been discussed with many gurus and philosophers that life is created to look good, feel better and to live longer. It is a process of constant struggle with reality, certainty and uncertainty of daily living. In realization, we have to face life as close as possible. We are only allowed to make decision and take action at a moment and at a place. As soon as we make a decision and take an action, we have to graciously and responsibly embrace its consequence and move on. Nothing lasts forever, but time, space and potentially religious eternal life.

Life is a journey filled with lessons. It encumbers hardships, heartaches, joys, celebrations and special moments with our loved ones and close friends. These encounters will ultimately lead us to our goal and purpose of life with many challenges. Such challenges will make us be tested with courage, weaknesses, strengths and lastly faith. How strong is our faith to face life? Everybody comes into our lives for some reasons or another. At times we take life for granted. We don't realize the seriousness of living a life here on earth.

But how many of us are able to do this. To ride a bicycle is easy as long as we are able to focus on our pedals, the road and to keep in balance.

In life, are we able to do that? It is not easy at all. Some of us will have that difficulty to adjust by loving others. At times in homes, workplace, we have our differences in opinions. We feel we have the right to our opinions and people around us should agree to our opinions. More often than not, we disagree among ourselves.

So we need to see ourselves in the Life-Loving. We need to focus what can be done to be satisfied in making such adjustments. In one saying: - : "Love yourself first and everything else fall in line. You really have to love yourself to get everything done in this world."

Not many of us are able to love ourselves. In fact, we hear around us that there are people who would say I hate myself, why must I be born into this family. Why? Why? Why am I born to be poor? Why am I born to be misunderstood?

Why am I not happy at all? I hate myself. I cannot love myself.

By loving ourselves, we will have that empowerment to love others.

As the scriptures say, 'Love one another as I have loved you.' This is the wisest saying to love others and give as much love you can give to others.

Thus by loving yourself first, there will be an aura in you that people will notice, that light shining in you that you cannot see but it is meant for others to notice that light. So live a life with no regrets, no matter what the problems are, - just let go.

Do have that warrior character with strength to love yourself. That's a hero in us, if we allow ourselves to notice that hero character. You need to see for yourself, what you say to yourself, how you feel about yourself and what actions you do for yourself will determine your destiny. To me it is sincerely truly from my heart I believe about loving yourself. We need to understand its full meaning of what loving yourself is. There is so much for you to understand about yourself and your life. And it is all good which in fact it is phenomenal. It is as though you are meant to have an amazing life that is to have everything you love and desire. In many areas of your life it could be your work which may be interesting or you are meant to accomplish a mission or other things you would love to accomplish.

Life-loving is meant to be loved on yourself, than with that love you can then radiate and pass on this amazing kind of love to others.

Love has been talked, discussed, brought up in our daily lives. Love has been written about since the beginning of time, in all religion, culture, traditions. It has been proclaimed by great thinkers, gurus, philosopher, prophets and other leaders of the world.

We need to have that power in us to be positive having good things in life and that is love which is truly the force of love. Love, is more than loving your family, friends and other favourite things which makes love to be the positive force thus empowering to carry on living with love. As the Scripture says in the gift of love that love is patient, love is kind, love is not envious or boastful arrogant or rude. It is not irritable or resentful, it does not rejoice in the wrongdoing, but rejoices in the truth. Love bears all things, believes all things, hopes all things and endures all things.

Isn't it amazing to think of love in us? Why not take a moment to ponder about love around us? What would the world become and be without love?

In the world today we live, look around us, watch the news on television, read the daily papers, what happen, why are there so many hardships, so much turmoil in terms of war, riots occur? Is there love in these places? I would say no. People tend to be selfish, wanting everything to themselves, take what that does not belong to them. There are homeless people around, poor housing. How can this be? Yes it can happen because there is no life-loving in many places and in our hearts. Love is the very force and power that can move us. We want to question ourselves why our life isn't amazing to live in harmony, living together. Why there are arguments here and there in the home, workplace and even in public places. We have this attitude living together with arguments and disagreement in opinions. This is because love does not exist in us at all. We tend to have our own minds and thoughts not thinking of others and giving way to others. We feel we can be kings having the power to control others. This is not love at all. There is no life-loving. We empower ourselves thinking we are better leaders than others.

Love is the very element and nature which can transfer to our family, our friends, co-workers, our neighbours.

So with life-loving, we should start from ourselves to smile, saying hello to those we meet, in the lift, in the park, in the mall. Yes, oh yes, if we were to greet others not knowing them, they think we are crazy or trying to take advantage of others, especially of the opposite gender. We need of course to be careful of when to greet or when is the time to say hello.

I knew of a close friend of mine years ago. Occasionally, we used to catch up to meet for some coffee or meals. Lately, when we met, I told him that I am embarking to write a book on Reflections of Life. He was so excited to hear from me. He requested me whether I could write about his life. He was willing to share his stories with me. My friend, Bernard now 60 years married, staying with his wife and daughter.

He said, "Richard I am very excited that you have decided to write a book. Can I be in it to share my life story? Any part of your chapters will do."

I replied, "Of course, if you are willing to share your life, your family life etc."

His father John was born in 1916 and his mother Jane in 1924. They met, got married in 1947. Bernard was the eldest in the family of eight – two boys and six girls.

His parents had never been separated from each other, even going shopping, marketing and doing things together. Of course, there were ups and downs between them. "My father, Bernard said, "would always give in to my mum."

This is Bernard's story.

"In June 1984, my mother with my other sisters went for a holiday in somewhere in Europe. They planned to stay with one of my married sister who migrated there to start a family. My mother was keen to visit her and to see the birth of her first grandchild. My father, one of my sister and I remained at home. During that year in 1984, I was planning to get an apartment. The apartment would be ready that same year."

He continued saying what his father said to him, "Son, can I come and live with you when your house is fully renovated and I hope you can take care of me as long as I live". Bernard replied in affirmative welcoming his father to stay with him when the apartment was ready.

I asked, "So what happen after that?"

"Well, during our conversation, he told me that he needed to go for a medical check-up and needed money to take a cab. I gave him ten dollars for the cab fare."

I asked, "So how was the medical check-up and medical result?"

Bernard started to sob somehow when I asked him such question. Bernard was quiet for a while, composing himself.

He continued, "Sometime in the evening of 4 June 1984, he called me from the hospital saying that he would be admitted into the ward for further observation and would be discharged the following day. He requested me to bring some new clothes and other things for him."

"I got into a cab with what he had asked me to bring to the hospital. Along the way to the hospital there was a traffic jam. During the journey, I felt queasy and my heart palpitated. I was wondering why this could happen. Spoke to the taxi driver, saying: "Driver can you go faster as I need to visit my father in the hospital." He replied: "I will try, mister, but the traffic is really heavy."

"Well, I reached my destination, went up to the ward my dad told me. However, I could not locate his bed. I walked round, made enquiries, saw some nurses running up and down." Bernard continued but his sobbing had begun to be louder. The nurse asked: "Are you Mr John's son? And I replied affirmatively."

She said: "I am sorry he passed on, that is the bed with the curtain cover up. She drew the curtain, and that was my father with his eyes open.

The nurse said: "Please make some arrangements and called your family members. Do close his eyes."

"I cried and called him to wake up. Eventually I closed his eyes, called my other relatives as my mum and sisters were away. I was frantic and didn't know what to do. I called my church members making enquiries for funeral service and arrangements."

"It was then that very morning (Europe time) I managed to call my mother and inform her of my father's passing.

Bernard sobbed louder still, but stopped for few minutes.

He said, "My mother and my sisters were about to leave home to do some sight-seeing.

"With such tragic news they took a connecting flight to return home". My father was laid to rest at home waiting for mum."

"Finally they arrived home. Mum was wailing throughout and I was there to witness her wailing. "Why can't you wait for me?" You promised that you wait until I return home. Why? Why? Can't you wait? Must you go and leave me behind."

Bernard continued "Of course, with her words like that I too couldn't take it and just went away to cry out. I was the only one at his bedside in the hospital."

"My father's wake was held for seven days as we had to wait for my two other sisters who were away to return home. During the wake, his friends came, spoke to me."

"Your dad was really something?" What did they mean?

"He came to the coffee shop with the ten dollars and gave us a treat, buying snacks and drinks," they said. "He told us that it might be the last time to eat and drink and we didn't believe him, saying such things to us."

"From here, I found out they mentioned that father was the life-loving, always giving to others. Through this conversation with his friends, I indeed cherished him in my heart for being a life-loving person."

So dear reader, from what you have read Bernard's family life story, to me his father was truly a life-loving person after all. Do you know anyone who is or was life-loving? Think about it, at times it is so difficult to understand people, some may be life-loving and some may not be at all. No matter what, you should try to be life-loving to others, shining out to others with your light, your life and be an example of life-loving. In this way, when others see you, they will notice that you are a life-loving person and they will cherish you for a long time.

On quotation from Saint Bernard of Clairvoux (1090-1153), Christian Monk and Mystic was "The measure of love is love with measure." This simply means about the love we have in us as what Rhonda Bryne in her book, mentioned when you're feeling joyful, you are giving joy and you'll receive back joyful experiences, joyful situations and joyful people, wherever you go. Having that life-loving in you will in turn make you rejoice, be happy, be the light and love for others to notice you. On the other hand, if you're feeling irritable, you're giving irritation to others and you'll receive back irritating situations and irritating people wherever you go.

So have that good feeling which will unite you with the force of love, because through this feeling of love, you will be a life-loving person. There will be feelings of excitement, feelings of passion, and feelings of enthusiasm.

Life is about moving forward toward a better tomorrow. It's up you to take the steps along the path you want for yourself and those you love. What you do and what you say have an impact on the people around as from the book "Moving Forward" by Dave Pelzer.

When hearing about Bernard's story and as I reflect about life and about the feelings of being a life-loving person, thoughts about a song of a father's love to his children. The song was 'Oh My Papa" by Eddie Fisher (1954). It is a song that I too experienced of my own father's love to me and my siblings.

In life-loving, love is unselfish as according to Scriptures that love is kind and patient. Love is patient with people and circumstances. It is in life-loving, we must endure all things all situations no matter how the difficulties are in our lives. So in life-loving to love others as we love ourselves, it means that love bears all things, believes all things which means give people the benefit of the doubt. Furthermore, love hopes all things for the best for all concerned and enduring. This is what love is all about. We should be able to love and try as much to make sacrifices to be able to take all in a stride in our lives.

Life-loving takes us up further in our steps of our lives. That is to know what we will go through and come what may that we are ready to accept the pains, the hardship to endure. If we are strong to surpassing such torments and allow love to flow in through our hearts, our minds and our souls, that love conquers all matters, then we are able to stand up straight and tall looking up and be proud that love really exists in our lives. Without love, we are nothing at all. The only thing that remains in our lives if we do not have experience life-loving, that there will be more hatred, more hardships and ever ready to fight back, retaliate to the other party which may be at home, at work or even outside of our home with neighbours and friends. So love doesn't insist on its own way; but give precedence and priorities to others, even if it has to compromise. Dave Pelzer again mentioned this.

Do you believe that your life is guided more by chance or by choice you've made? What impact has either one made on your life thus far?

Remember in life sometimes you only get one chance, that one chance to connect, one chance to make a difference in your life and others. Only one chance! Don't we all live life for the simple desire to be happy?

With so much love in us, we can exude that kind of light of love to others. By loving others no matter in what circumstances they are in, we are able to profess the love to them. They may be in situations of helplessness, in dire straits of problems and meaningless life they encounter, if we understand these circumstances and empathize with them, the love in us will bring out the brightness of love and tranquillity to them. With such love-light transmission, all the situations and circumstances will just dissipate and disappear from their lives. They will be able to receive your life-loving attitude and definitely with their positive change of life, they too will transmit that life-loving to others.

Isn't true that all of us have gone through obstacles in our lives? Day in, day out, we face obstacles and problems in life. This has brought us to a standstilll. There are people who have experienced one failure after another and feel unable to keep going.

We should all share our visions no matter how small they are. By doing so, we will discover the purpose in life. With love, dream big dreams. Tell people your dreams with enthusiasm, they will support you and encourage you to go for it, even to an extent support you to set your goal to greater heights.

What you see for yourself, what you say to yourself, how you feel about yourself and what actions you do for yourself will determine your destiny. Achieve that life-loving for yourself. Your life's challenges and experiences are directing and guiding you to do something truly magnificent with your life.

In life-loving, you need to have that exuberance in your daily life. This means to exude the love, the light and the aura within you to allow others receive that exuberance in you. It is important that you too send out the signal of this emotion, this life-loving so that others will see that light of love.

So what does Life-loving means? It is in Mother Teresa various quotes and some of them are my favourite, "Life is an opportunity, benefit from it", Life is a challenge, meet it", "Life is a struggle, accept it." In actual fact Life-loving is everything in us. It is the characteristic, the behaviour, the attitude, the emotion, your physique, your whole human being that will exude the life-loving in you to others you meet. In Mother Teresa's quotation it said – "Every time you smile at someone, it is an action of love, a gift to that person, a beautiful thing."

All of us if you know it have the power to love unlimitedly. We need to activate love, not just to fulfil our purpose but to be involved for the world to have peace and fulfilment in life. Thus it is important to value our lives in having the life-loving attitude to spread the inner being of us, the very essence of our love to everyone especially at home, our spouses, children, parents and friends at work and social. You may find it at times difficult to handle with difficult situation, but move forward one step at a time, day by day. Rest assured there will be valuable lessons learned and gaining strength each day. By doing so without giving up to love people in life-loving, peace will come your way into your heart. Be always ready to welcome those in need with open arms to say 'I care', 'I listen', 'I feel for you'. Sometimes these words you say may not be for some who are in distress. Some will welcome those soothing words and would say 'thank you'. Nothing will make you feel down than living without purpose of whatever you do that is to have the gift of love that gives you joy and makes your life meaningful. In this way, you have already achieved that life-loving. This then is the greatest gift. So be patient.

As long as you can hold on to that passion of life-loving, rest assured that you will not lose heart and faith in reaching out to others. However, do remember that having this life-loving passion can come with risk. Risk is meant to be there whenever you are willing to be strong showing empathy and having that compassion for others.

Don't worry or stress about the next few hours. Forget about tomorrow as tomorrow has its own troubles. Don't think about the past. Yesterday's gone into the air. Flush out the unneeded stress. Too much worrisome you will make yourself be sick and down with ill-health. Which type of person are you- the worry one or having the best day of your life to enjoy and giving.

This very essence of love is very unique if we know the fundamental issues of spreading the love to others so that those we meet along the way will notice that special kind of a person you are in the universe. With the life-loving in us, we also must that faith to put in action that will work. As Nick said in his book, all we need to do is put faith into action by reaching out to those who love you, those who want to help you.

I have experienced a kind of exercise that has really helped me to be more positive in reflecting my daily living. It is a simple exercise that I hope you too will do to be more life-loving. So dear reader, if you can do it so that you will be more life-loving in your daily life.

The gift of love is in each and every one of us. That gift is in our hearts, our minds and our soul. Only thing is that not many of us realise this gift in us. A song that I appreciate is the "The Gift of Love".

What does it mean – "The profit soon turns strangely dim." To me it means, that whatever we do without the love within us, we gain from others may just dissipate into thin air. And we don't see the thankfulness, the gratitude, the appreciation to be considered as the profit, not in terms of monetary values but in sacrificial and time values.

Allow me, dear reader in a simple exercise, a simple thank you to yourself, for your whole being. Follow the steps carefully. Do it in the morning when you wake up and again before you sleep.

The steps in the morning are:-

Step One:-

Say 'thank you' to your mind, your brain. This word will help you to be more alert. It will make you feel for exhilarating in the morning and refresh for the day.

Step Two:-

Say 'thank you' to your eyes. Your eyes are the windows of love, the windows of light. By saying this word, it allows you to see more light, more refreshing environment as you move along the path of happiness in your home, your workplace and among your loved ones and friends.

Step Three:-

Say 'thank you' to your ears. Your ears are the passages of hearing good news and not negative words or even gossips from people. By doing so to say thank you, it will block all negative feelings.

Step Four:-

Say 'thank you' to your mouth, your tongue. Your mouth and tongue are meant to speak good words and good wishes and not to slander or saying untoward feelings to others. Your mouth and tongue are meant to greet and praise people even some of them may have ill-feelings towards you. It doesn't matter about such circumstances so just do it by acknowledging saying thank you to them. Ultimately this will surprise those, why don't you hit back by saying nasty words to them, so don't retaliate.

Step Five:-

Say 'thank you' to your heart by placing your right hand on it. Let the thank you has the deep impression in your heart. Your heart will accept this thank you. In doing so, your heart will soften and not be harden trying to hate people but to love them all the more. Your heart will be strengthened and your heartbeat will be very regular and not palpitating.

Step Six:-

Say 'thank you' to your hands. Your hands are creating to help and bring people up when they are down and not to hit. Your hands are meant to serve others by delivering good gestures in hand-shaking and welcoming people no matter who they are. They can be rich, poor or homeless, so welcome them.

Step Seven:-

Say' thank you' to your legs. These legs are made for walking to help those in need. Your legs can be athletic, can run to those in need of help when crisis arises. Your legs are made to move about in proper motion and quicken steps when are needs to succumb.

Step Eight:-

Finally, say 'thank you' to your whole being, your whole body. Your humanness is very important by saying thank you. Your body will be rejuvenated, be more healthier, more robust to move along and be part of the community you are in. Your whole body will be protected from any kind of illnesses if you do take care of your body, by eating healthily in terms of proper nutrition.

Before you retire to bed at night, you can repeat the above steps. However, it will be the reverse way. By saying 'thank you' to your body parts, do end up by a second thank you that the day has been good to you. Even if you have a bad day, it doesn't matter, continue to say thank you and pray that the next day will be better for you, that you will experience a brighter day. I have experienced a bad day too, at times wanting to give up, thinking of taking revenge on those who hurt, preparing it for the following day. However, I restrain myself and ignore the negative attitude and say thank you. The moment I did that, all the negativity of my hurt feelings, my unhappiness gone, taking in the positivity for the day. Finally, as you about to fall asleep, take a deep breath. Breathe in positivity and breathe out negativity. Positivity is the word for all positive attitudes and behaviour. Negativity is the just the opposite. Do these breathing exercises a few times until your eyes will become heavier letting you to be in the rapid eye movement into a deep sleep. I assure you dear reader it can work, and if you faithfully, religiously continue to do so.

Again in Mother Teresa's quote: "Do not think that love in order to be genuine has to be extraordinary. What we need is to love without getting tired. Be faithful in small things because it is in them that your strength lies."

This is really in the life-loving if you have tried your best to perform throughout your whole entire life. If you haven't done so to have that life-loving in you, it is not too late to start anew. If you have done so throughout, continue to do so for life-loving and you will blossom fulfilling with so much love sharing with others around – your family, spouses, friends and colleagues.

We must never forget that we are born to be life-loving. We are created into this world to be life-loving to others. However, mankind tends to be more selfish when things go wrong and we only think as it is each man is for himself.

Selfishness and the evilness of this world have eaten us up and creep into our systems, our body and soul. We feel that is alright to be ourselves, our own selfishness and we should earn this through our own means. It is not wrong to earn our living through our own means. But it is wrong to earn through our selfish attitude and to ignore others who may be in need. To live a life-loving attitude is to try to acknowledge others, to assist others whenever there is a need to do so. No wonder there is turmoil and upheaval in this world from the beginning of life till today. Man against man, country against country, government against government. There is no end to this kind of living. We tend to feel that it is our right to live and just ignore not to bother other people. Let them live their own life whether they are needy, helpless or homeless. Not only it happens in the world, but it also happens in our very backyard, among our family members, relatives and even our closest friends. Family members, friends can betray one another for the sake of selfishness and by achieving this we say it is only right that we assume to have our own way of life. No, it is not to be this way. It meant to have that life-loving to have it back into our life, to nurture and make it grow into us, to bloom ever so brightly this life-loving behaviour and attitude. Only then with this life-loving blossoming in us, we can really feel that loving kindness and this will make us very happy and life fulfilling in us.

It is important to be the best you can be. In Ralph Waldo Emerson's quote (Essayist & Philosopher), he said: "Make the most of yourself for that is all there is to you." So count your blessings. Be thankful what you have in your life and not to be over-zealous. Do not envy others who may have more things than you. Think of those who have not. Do not behave to have more things in life by comparing with others who have more than you. This kind of living does not make you a life-loving person at all. It is cruel to behave having such thoughts. Life-loving is meant to bring you peace, more love, more care and concern for others in your home, your workplace and the environment you live it. One more thing, life-loving also means to care not only to humans but to animals as well. Be more loving to the animals and see the beauty of God's creation in them.

Some of them may be ferocious, some docile, some tame. That is how God created them to be. Even animals have instinct. To them life-loving may not be in them as they are meant to live, to survive in this world, thus they will fight for their own food for their young and for their kind.

Bernard was all ready to share more of his experience with his father when he was alive.

He said, "My father was somewhat very prayerful man. He would say his evening prayers without fail. He would invite his children to join in with mum. Of course, mum always joined in. We children, at times, reluctantly joined in. Father didn't force us to join in. Only twice a year, he would emphasise requesting us to join and that was at Christmas and New Year's Eve at midnight."

"He had so much of life-loving to his children. He would put others first before self. He taught me a lot of life-loving. He said to me once as far as I remembered during one festive occasion: This was what he said to me. "Son, you are the eldest in the family. Show love to your younger ones. When you get married and have own family with children, be what I am to all of them leading a prayerful life. Well, as the years go by, I felt so decline and slacken in my prayer life. I have not practiced well to what my father had said to me."

Bernard felt apprehensive to share further. During our conversation, I asked him was there anything he would like to continue sharing about his encounter with his father.

He then continued looking down trying to hold back his tears. Eventually he cried and this was what he said.

"I cried so much when seeing my father passed away like that." I didn't really all my life as I grow up to say I love him. He cried and cried. I held his hands. His sharing touched me and really empathise him.

"I remembered during my church camp a song was played as **"The Living Years" (1988) by Mike & the Mechanics**.

It is true to what Bernard had experienced about life in the Living Years.

So I appeal to all children, parents to really ponder on the words and understand its true meaning. It will be too late when we die, to admit we don't see eye to eye. At times we live with regrets in not saying what we want to say – to express the love we have got to each other. Do we listen to each other? At times yes, but most times, we hear but do not listen. Our ears only want to hear what is being said and we only listen to gossips and bad news but not the good news of saying 'I love you" kind of expression.

To have this life-loving, there must be a positive flow and we need to follow the positive flow. We have that interconnectedness and intuition to love others choosing which directions to take and which opportunities to follow. Keeping your decision in harmony with the underlying flow of your life creates a feeling of positive movement and joy.

This is I believe so. By having the intuition in our life and making a right decision, our life-loving would be an added advantage to uphold our integrity, our character, our attitude and behaviour. It said further in the book that the intuitive way is to see that you've noticed something is missing from your life. Last year you were not thinking about it and now you are. Something in you is opening to a relationship. There is an inner urge, giving you that motivation. It is in you to find that life-loving, to know that there are others who are in need of life-loving relationship.

There was once a story of a working mother I heard when I was younger during my school days. She had a son of about 4 years old. This son was very independent and lovable. One day the son saw his mother working so hard every day, coming home to prepare dinner for him and other siblings. He said, "Mommy works so hard. I think I will surprise her when she returns home today."

Well, mother returned home, preparing dinner. She looked stressed after a hard day's work. She rushed to prepare dinner for her family. Her son came in to the kitchen. He said, "Mommy, I have a surprise for you. Look, beautiful flowers plucked from our garden and I place them in this beautiful vase. It is for you."

Guess what did the mother do? She screamed at her son. "You know I am busy and here you plucked from the garden and place in my favourite vase for me. Now get out. I am busy." The son was taken aback and cried. He dropped the vase and the flowers went down spreading over the kitchen floor. The mother screamed again, "Look, what you have done, giving me extra burden to clean up.'

The son ran off, feeling down, miserable and disappointed. If you have such a child, what would you have done dear reader? When I heard this story, I felt so hurt. What kind of a mother is this? Can't she feel grateful, thankful and have that life-loving for her son? Well, the son went off to his room, prayed and even asked God to forgive his mother for such behaviour. You know what he said? 'God, forgive mommy, please. She might not understand my feeling for her. I know she is tired and really work very hard for us to earn more money. I am sorry God that I thought by doing this act, would make her happy. Guess I was wrong doing at the wrong time. Maybe, I will do so next time when mommy is calm and resting after dinner." At the same time, his mother came into the room. She heard him praying loudly. She cried. She went in hugged her son and said sorry to him. She didn't know that this precious son, so lovable and clever to think of such an act as such a young age.

So life-loving is really important to all of us. Always be appreciative to others who have kind and caring thoughts for us. Always be life-loving to others and such an act will return to us in plentiful and bountiful ways.

What Donald Aftmar said in his book on the Mindfulness Code that if you truly want to change your life, you must first be willing to change your mind. It requires using the mind to look inward and observe its own workings.

Love needs action. We need not talk about love, but we need to show actions. We need to walk the talk about love, and not talking. It means walking the talk and not talking the walk.

Love opens to all. At times there are people who stay for a short time on earth that end up making a lasting impression not only in our lives, but in our hearts as well. Of course, there are people such as Mahatma Ghandi, Mother Teresa and others who on this earth shown so much love to others. These are the people who show love before self. They put others before self. This is the love action and not the love talk.

Love flows in all parts of our body- it a love story that continues day after day, in fact your whole life. You are a walking, talking story of love. This means the love story is part of a large love story, no matter how big or small, the love story is endless. Thus by seeing other love stories in other people's lives, be it they are poor, homeless, frail elderly or even your loved ones at home, spouse, children, parents, the love stories never end and will always continue until we depart from Mother Earth. Even when we are gone, the love stories still continue because we still love those who were gone and remember them in our hearts. This is the story of love. In actual fact, the love of life leads us to help others simply it makes us feel good and great to contribute to those around us – our friends, family, colleagues and even strangers for that matter.

Only in love you have the ability to share what you have – your wealth or even your possessions and knowledge. You may have much to give or you may have little to give, the key to the power of giving is to your potential.

> **"There is always enough for the needy,**
> **but never enough for the greedy."**
> **Mahatma Ghandi.**

So start giving yourself, your family and community. Start to love as love is the most powerful force in the world.

By giving people your respect, you will display through active listening. This is to start with yourself, learn to accept yourself and love yourself before you embark to love others with your own capacity.

Life-Giving

"The emotions must be called upon to give feeling to the thought so it will take form."
Charles Haanel (1866-1949), New Thought Author

In Life-Giving – the questions you may put forward "What do you do that is life-giving for you?" It is in the text of Journey With Me (<u>http://journeywithme.infor/</u>).

By this it is meant what do you do that brings nourishment to your soul?

Sometimes our life can be so messy, so crammed in doing things that we don't realise the most important we should have done in this Life-Giving way. We only think for ourselves so much that we tend to forget others in our daily life. We tend to focus so much of what we should do or shouldn't do at all. We need to relax and see around us who needs this life-giving. It could be our loved ones at home, people at work, the homeless, the poor, the underprivileged living in our own very backyard, our neighbourhood, in our community.

Whenever I can, I would devote myself to do volunteer work in some fund raising projects in the community. The event can be Flag Day, Charity Walk or any other fund raising projects. In life-giving situation, we have to look at ourselves, what have we done or what we have not done to fulfil this life-giving to others. Mother Teresa again in her quote said this: "At the end of life we will be judged by not how many diplomas we have received, how much money we have made, how many great things we have done. We will be judged by "I was hungry, and you gave me something to eat, I was naked and you clothed me. I was homeless, and you took me in." This very nature is true to practice the life-giving. Although it isn't easy to do so, but at least try to have within your home, your family to show that life-giving is somewhat a beautiful thing to understand and easy to practice in terms showing the love you have to others. When you feel that life-giving in you, and decide to share with others, this life-giving will illuminate in your heart. Your heart will come to understand that you are ready to bring out the life-giving to others around you. We also need to do this to ourselves in life-giving. We need to have it within ourselves and understand the importance of life-giving by saying – yes, I will have life-giving in me, with this life-giving say it and clearly in your heart, your mind that life-giving is a natural thing to share with others. By repeating the words – "'Life-giving in me come easy, life-giving will help me to nurture myself, I will have life-giving with all my heart, I will say life-giving is in me always and will never leave me."

The definition of life-giving is having the power of providing sustenance, spirit or life. The energy that a mother expends when she is giving birth to baby

Is an example of life-giving. Bernard was so eager to continue sharing his life experience as I decided to start another chapter on life-giving. This is his story.

"I met my wife in mid-1980 through some night studies. We went on dates and eventually got married in 1982. Well, as it is said when couples got hitched, next thing is about children. It came to naught that we didn't have any just after marriage. Somehow, we lived together blissfully.

Then something just happened as you can call it faith and really life-giving. In May of 1991, we went to a church attended a procession. We were among the congregation watching the procession. We met a priest during the procession and he said, "Why don't you come along with the other congregation following the procession." We at first declined the invitation. He said again, "Do it and you will have a child the following year." We looked at each other rather perplexed and said ok why not and give it a try then. I carried the statute stand end holder among the other helpers. My wife walked close to me. The procession ended entering the church and it was over. That same year sometime in July, we with among our friends went on a pilgrimage retreat to Malaysia. It was Saint Ann's Feast Day.

On the way to the retreat, my wife mentioned that she was unwell and felt queasy in her stomach like having a lump. I told her to pray and asked for healing, perhaps seek intercession that the lump might change to be a foetus. We returned home after the two days retreat. Eventually she went for a medical check-up. I went to work. During the afternoon, she called that the doctor said she was in her third month of pregnancy. I was dumbfounded. This was really life-giving to us. It was really ecstatic.

As the months went by, I became like a pregnant father instead of her. My wife always had problems in walking around and working, knocking at things and didn't feel any hurt around her tummy. I told her to be careful that the child was precious and life-giving to us. As we went along our daily task at work and at home, one evening after dinner we strolled along the path just below our block. Somehow a very instinct came over me and told her to walk along the path and I near the grass verge. We argued about it as it was always me walking on the outside and she nearby the grass verge. Subsequently, she agreed that I walked nearby the grass verge. Lo! and behold, as I walked, I slipped, stepped on an orange peel. I fell and was like sliding about less than one meter. My right leg hurt so much because my knee cap was dislocated and almost went below my thigh. I screamed in pain. Of course, what my wife did - called for help. Neighbours heard our cry, one brought a pillow down to allow to rest my head on it. Police was summoned. Police thought I committed suicide falling from the tenth floor window. I said it was ridiculous, I would have died already. Ambulance came and brought me to a nearby hospital. Again something happened, while in the ambulance, I prayed ceaselessly, seeking for intercession. In the ambulance it was so happen the air-conditioner broke down. Upon arrival at the hospital, I was wheeled into the observation ward. Again something happen. The air-conditioner in the ward also broke down too. It was so hot and I was in pain. About two hours later, the doctor came to examine me. He asked: "What is wrong with you?" You had a bad fall? Relax and calm down. He felt my right leg and said: "There is nothing wrong with you at all!" I told him that my right knee was dislocated and he answered it was in the right position. He said: "Ok we will send you for X-ray and see how". I went for X-ray and the result was that I had a hair-line crack and it was not serious at all.

Amazing isn't it? This was really life-giving when you make a decision to have that faith in you and just go for it without even thinking about the consequences after. This was how Bernard felt. He continued, "My wife was in her sixth month and so on till February 1992, she felt queasy and the feeling of about to give birth and the time was about 11 pm. We rushed to the hospital. She was admitted and

I waited outside. She was supposed to have a normal birth delivery. She was in labour pain for almost eight hours."

"Doctor informed me that she had to go for caesarean instead. Then around 5.30 am she gave birth to a beautiful baby girl. I called my mother to tell her the good news and that was around 6am. She woke up to hear the news but broke down. I asked the reason. She said: "Your father came down to me in my dream. He was holding a baby in his arms and told me – Dear, take this child, it is your grandchild. I told him to take it back and where in the world did he get the child. He said again to take it and put in my arms and he left."

"My mother told me that as she woke up, she was holding a bolster like as though she was carrying a child in her arms. This brought tears to us and we experienced the life-giving. We had yet to decide in naming the child. Some names came up and nothing fit this beautiful baby. Then it struck us, hey since it was such a graciously heavenly gift, we shall name her Ann. She was born on 11 February, the feast of Our Lady of Lourdes. The name was dedicated to St Ann when we went for the retreat.

Dear reader, it was a tremendous experience for Bernard and his wife. I felt so much for him daring to share his story. Till this day, I will never forget such a wonderful experience in life-giving for Bernard and his family.

As we live in our daily lives, we must understand the meaning of life-giving. Is life-giving only giving away material needs to others? No. In life-giving, we must learn to live with it and share with others the life-giving experience in our lives, no matter whether it was in the past or recent years. We need to have the fulfilment of life-giving. Others will see the inside of us that light which will illuminate shining beyond our understanding and knowledge. Only those who are close to us and living with us or even others in workplace or anywhere, will notice that we have the life-giving character. It is not too late to have the experience of life-giving neither will it hinders us to have life-giving if we were to grasp its meaning in totality. Full commitment is needed to grasp and hold it close in our heart that life-giving is somewhat natural and we can nurture this life-giving to grow in us to become better person in terms of character, behaviour, wisdom and be more loving to others without rejecting anyone whoever he or she is be it rich, poor, homeless or persons with special needs. We should accept everyone as it is. Where there is life-giving there is love around us.

Well, it has been almost so many years in our present century till today. The life-giving is still within us. However, of course in every marriage, there are ups and downs, gibbering, disagreements and arguments here and there. But with life-giving, one partner has to take it in a stride to be cool, calm and relax. By being docile to the other partner's needs, definitely, the disagreement will end and we will be together living in harmony and peace at home with the fulfilment of life-giving.

Another part of Bernard's experience in life-giving was his sister who was a life-giving person throughout her life. Amanda was her name

"She died in 2010, the month of September. Amanda had this character in being obedient to others especially to my mother. Whenever there was a task or chore to do, she was asked to do so. Amanda not one in her moments would complain, she would comply to do the chores requested by my mother or even her siblings. One day, as I was at home with them (mother, Amanda and our domestic caregiver), my mother with her early dementia, she was misbehaving in saying nasty things about someone, Amanda would then cajole us (me and the caregiver) to be calm, to be there for her, soothing her. Amanda even told me and the caregiver to accept the fact that mother was aging and may not know what she was saying at all. She meant no harm. She didn't mean what she said. This as far as I remember, was really life-giving that Amanda could think so far ahead. You see Amanda was intellectually challenged. It may seem she was born this way or so as mother did not tell us so. Amanda could read and write simple words only. She understood fully well what was said and was not cognitively impaired at all.

One day, Amanda had a fall through her style of walking. She had inner stroke which was undetected only when she was diagnosed with Parkinson at the age of 57. She had difficulty in her mobility. She needed to be handhold when walking around. At times she could and at other times she could not. Our domestic helper, Missy used to take care of both of them – mother and Amanda. One day as I visited mother, I invited three of them to go out for a walk to have meals together. They were so used to Missy taking care of them. At that time, mother needed handhold to walk. We went down to the ground level. I took mother's hand and walk, while Missy took Amanda's hand. Mother refused to move and just stood still.

"I said, "Mum, let's walk, come go for dinner." She replied, "Call the girl, come here hold hand." So Missy came to take mother's hand. I went forward took Amanda's hand. Eventually, Amanda too refused to walk. She turned back, look back and saw Missy hold mother's hand. Amanda too wanted to have Missy with her. In the end, Missy hold both of them, one on the right and the other on the left and I was left with no one walking with me.

This also I would say, Missy has that life-giving to both of them. She had shown so much life-giving that eventually made them to accept Missy.

At the later stage of Amanda's life, her Parkinson illness had taken control of her. She could not walk as she would before. She would fall for no apparent reason as her legs were unsteady. She would undress herself at home in full view of others and would just lie on the floor. Her body was thwarted forward and would sway to the left and right sometime. This was a very stressful moment for Massie to take care of mother and Amanda at the same time. At this stage, mother's dementia was in the middle stage. Amanda's mobility became so bad, her speech was slurring. She was not in the right frame of mind. She starred at others blankly. Her eyes were blurry, not knowing what she was looking. Her voice became softer and was inaudible. At the final stage with her bad fall, she had cataract too. She had problems in eating and swallowing. Whatever food places in front of her she would gobble the food up. At this stage, she needed tube feeding through her nose or through the opening of her throat. She needed serious nursing care. She was eventually admitted to a nursing home. When she became seriously ill, she was discharged from the nursing home and admitted to hospital as she had difficulty in breathing. She was put on oxygen. We visited her daily. Mother would also visit her. Mother still recognised Amanda and requested that Amanda should go home. One evening, mother became impatient and requested to go home earlier around 9 pm. Missy and I said good-night to Amanda, touching her hands. At that moment, Missy mentioned that Amanda waved her left hand and perhaps suggested not to go as yet. I told Missy, mother needed rest. As soon as we reached home at around 11pm, hospital called to return that Amanda's condition was unstable. We rushed back, all of us, but Missy and mother stayed at home. As soon as we reached, Amanda was gone.

With Bernard's sharing, I could feel the life of Amanda in her life-giving. According to Bernard, during her lifetime, she portrayed so much of life-giving until the time she passed on. Her simplicity, her way of life touches people around her. Everyone she met at below the block or in the neighbourhood, she would smile at everyone with her simple gesture of greetings. During the wake, one elderly man, living upper floors, he was surprised that Amanda a sweet lovable person and kind would just die like that.

Bernard continued, "He and I exchange greetings during the wake, introducing ourselves." The man said, "Amanda was so sweet, kind and helpful. I an old man used to buy grocery from the supermarket nearby and with heavy load, she happened to pass by, offer her help to carry for me to my home. What a wonderful sweet loving person she was, always give to others her helping hand."

Yet another story of Amanda for her life-giving in her life took place. During the wake too, an elderly lady came by saw the photo of Amanda was taken aback and could not believe that she passed away. She paid respect and wept for a while. She said, "Every time I look out at the kitchen window, saw Amanda walking around below the block, she would look up, saw me and waved at me. This had been going on for some time. She would even ask whether I needed help to buy things for me at the supermarket. I lived two floors up from where Amanda lived. She would said out loudly – want to buy things, want to buy food, I come and buy for you. Each time I replied thank you, it is ok, you are very kind." At this stage, again the lady wept.

"That Richard was the reason I want to share about Amanda's life to you." said Bernard. "Not only she had that life-giving, she had the life-loving attributes too."

Dear reader, try to see the connection of the two- Life-loving and Life-giving. It is intertwined. Without life-loving, you will not experience life-giving at all. We need to be more altruistic to be able to understand others, why there are people not being the same as you, in terms of behaviour, character and attitude. Altruism or selflessness is the principle or practice of concern for the welfare of others. No two snowflakes are alike. We are made differently. By being different from each other, we are able to experience life-loving and then will be able to have the experience in life-giving. Actually, the life-giving is in all of us. It is only a matter for us to realise it.

Some may experience life-giving at early stages of life, while others may experience in later stage of life. Some also may experience it in much later years perhaps in the sixties, seventies or even later. No matter at what stage we experience it, it is not too late to practice and to have that attitude of life-giving. The most important thing is to be happy, to be able to understand life-giving. We need to be selfless at times in order to have this life-giving. By helping and serving others, putting others before self, we will experience a good karma. When we do it, always remember what goes around will come around. So life-giving has the good karma in us. On the other hand, some at times may not experience life-giving although we have in us, we tend to have the life-giving to ourselves which means, what we have, we have for ourselves only and not for others. This will then be a bad karma.

Bernard said, "My sister Amanda all her life had the good karma. She was very simple in her life. Whatever that she has in her own possession of her things, she would gladly share with others even though how little she had. This was at that time she was healthy, her mobility was excellent and was able to self-care".

"Even during her illness, she would also gladly share things with others. She was that jubilant, cheerful and led a very simple life. Her child-like behaviour would draw children to her very easily as she loved children. Amanda was that kind of person I would describe having the life-loving and life-giving experience till the very end of her life."

I came across a song or rather a hymn – "When Love Is Found." It was sung when I attended a Church service on Sunday.

The lyrics had a strong sense of meaning about love. When love is found and hope comes home….. Isn't it good to know that only when love is found we will also have the life-loving intertwined with life-giving because addition to the lyrics, it said when love has flowered in trust and care, build both each day that love may dare as we reach beyond homes warmth and light to serve and strive for truth and right. Yes, only with love at home with so much warmth and light, we are able to exude the life-loving, life-giving to others especially at home.

By having karma is when people treat you is their karma; how you react is yours. You get what you give, whether it's bad or good. According to Kadampa Buddhism, the law of karma is a special instance of the law of cause and effect, according to which all our actions of body, speech and mind are causes and all our experiences are their effects. On karma, every action we perform leaves an imprint or potentiality on our very subtle mind. Each imprint eventually gives rise to its own effect.

> *"Be careful of your moods and feelings, for*
> *there is an unbroken connection between*
> *your feelings and your visible world."*
> *Neville Goddard (1905-1972)*

Law of attraction states that in responding to you if you think and feel whether your thoughts and feelings are good or maybe bad, you are still giving them out. By so doing, they will return to you as you have given out automatically. So by being good to others, you will receive goodness. It means that if you change your life by changing your thoughts and feelings, having positive thoughts and feelings, your entire life will change for the better. It is by cultivating that life-giving in you. So go on move forward, don't look back of the past, be yourself for today for life-giving, you never what know lies in the future.

In life-giving, every good feeling will unite you with the force of love. This is because love is the essence of all good feelings. By having that life-giving, you will have that enthusiasm, excitement and passion from love.

Remember that law of attraction says whatever you give, you receive. It is in the law of attraction with kind of boomerang and an echo, whatever you do it will come back to you in terms of what you have done. What you give in measure will come back to you in the same measure. So if your life-giving to others giving out with great measures, you will receive in greater measures, a thousand-fold of good things in life. So Give It – Receive It.

"To believe in the things you can see and touch is no belief at all; but to believe in the unseen is a triumph and a blessing."
Abraham Lincoln (1809-1865)
16th President of the United States.

To give is to love in the simple way of life. It will return to you in the relationship and in your whole entire life. That is how easy it is to give love through kindness, gratitude and passion. Having that intimacy, loving and caring power we can improve relationship with our family, close friends. This then is about the sources of deepest joy in our lives.

"A hundred times every day I remind myself that my inner and outer life depend on the labours of other men, living and dead, and that I must exert myself in order to give in the same measure as I have received and am still receiving."
Albert Einstein – Nobel Prize Winner

What you give to others, you give to yourself. So for life-giving, give love to others through kindness, support, encouragement, gratitude or other good feeling. By doing so, the goodness will come back to you in full measure, multiple receive, bringing love to every other area of your life, including health, wealth, happiness and career. If you give negativity feeling to others, through any means of criticism, anger, impatience or any kind of bad feeling such as talking or gossiping back about others in a negative attitude, you will receive negativity ill-will. This will then affect your entire life in terms of health and other illness and perhaps unhappiness in your life.

You can tell what kind of relationship you are in and what're you giving. If you give what is good to others, you will receive good from others too.

Buddha is his writing said:

> **"You will not be punished for your anger, but you will be punished by your anger."**

In life-giving, we should try our utmost best to learn how to give ourselves to others in terms of services without even saying what I give to others they must return the same favour or else I will be angry and not helping anymore in future. So getting angry is fruitless, thus should know what Buddha quoted about anger.

The relationship is life-giving you have with family members and close friends are going to be the most important source of happiness in your life. We need to take stock of ourselves to be careful showing concern for one another to come into terms that in any relationship with one another will be better.

Thus, Dale Carnegie quoted: **"If we think happy thoughts, we will be happy. If we think miserable thoughts, we will be miserable."**

> **"Anyone in their right mind would choose peace and joy instead of suffering. Awareness is the key."**
> -Sonia Ricotti (Unsinkable, 2011)

Victor Frankl said that it's the last of all human freedom, the ability to choose. So we can choose to look at whatever we want or we can look and choose taking the wrong path.

Having bad thoughts such as hate, anger or resentment toward another person is something comparable in taking poison.

You may have so much to give to anyone around you in life-giving. Those who are blessed with education and knowledge bear the responsibility of sharing their advantages with others. If we do not use these gifts we are given, we lose them. If we use the gifts to make a difference, we enhance them, increasing our knowledge and abilities. So give to yourself, your family and community. One of the best gifts you can give to people is your respect, display through active listening.

So, when to give, when to love? It is today, now at this very moment. No hesitation at all. Do not think twice. Do it now.

Where to give – the three areas:-

Your emotions, values and motivations

Your skills and other resources you have to give in terms of time, conditions and so on.

Giving is a beautiful experience. By practicing giving, you can make a big difference to others and in your life. You will be a much happier person today if you do it NOW!

We ask what life is, as we continue to live in our daily lives. It is a life-giving. By giving to others, we have life in us. We are living in a world of beauty, but few of us open our eyes to see it! Yes, what different place this world would be if we have the ability to see and to hear.

I read the life of Saint Francis of Assisi on the reflection on insensitivity to the beauty and wonderful things in the environment we live in. The story said about him and a monk desired to preach in a village. On the way, Saint Francis, saw a dog in the town, helped a poor woman across a street, stopped to see the wonder of the town and the place. He spoke with love so kindly to all the people he met. Knowing that he and the monk needed quickly to preach, the monk said, "Master we need to hurry and to preach to the people." Saint Francis replied, "We have done so already. We went about preaching here in this village square, loving people, patting the dog, spoke to the villagers and this is life. That was of itself a sermon."

This moved me dear readers. Preaching itself is meaningless if there are no actions from our part. Life is like that. Life is meaningless, if we do not show love to others with care and concern. Life becomes lifeless. We do not have life in us. Life-giving is useless, if we do not show our love to others, especially to our neighbours, loved ones and also to animals.

Life-Radiance

What is the meaning of radiance? In the Chambers Dictionary, radiant – sending out rays of light or heat, glowing, beaming with joy – example he or she has a radiant smile.

So to me, radiance is exactly what it means, bringing smiles to everyone we meet, be at home with loved ones, in our workplace, on the streets to the man in the street, everywhere. Life-radiance is the way to everyone's heart. It is the way that will make everyone gleaming, happy that there are people who always smile radiantly. In some of the philosophy and psychology books, writers would always expound on giving happiness to others by simply smiling to them. Greetings with a smile are always the first before we say our greetings like welcome, good morning and so on with other forms of greetings even in handshakes.

Why is life-radiance a topic in Reflections of life? It simply means that when we smile radiantly, we are able to experience the life-loving and life-giving at the same time. Isn't it wonderful to have life-radiance in us too?

Bernard knew that my next chapter is Life-Radiance. Here he mentioned to me.

"During her days on her from young to adulthood, Amanda would easily portray her life-radiance by smiling to everyone she meets along the way. Her greetings to those she met, would melt their hearts and in return those who seen her smiles, would eventually smile back at her automatically. Her smile was really infectious. Whenever I took mum and

Amanda out just for a meal or even a walk with Missy the caregiver, I noticed Amanda would smile especially to the elderly and young children on the streets. When I visited mum at home after work in the evening, Amanda would readily open the door and greeted me with simple hello and then smile. She would also ask me whether I have taken my dinner."

Try to remember a moment when you were touched by someone so beautiful that your heart could barely contain it. That moment could be when someone, your loved one, your colleagues, friends or a stranger smile at you so radiantly that it has made you remember that moment of smile when you reciprocate the smile to that person. Imagine that kind of greeting so wonderfully radiant during that moment and that make you experienced that moment more fully. This is if you are unaware it is the gift of life-loving, life-giving and life-radiance, all three in one. Without that first two - life-loving, life-giving you would not experience life-radiance at all. Also life-radiance is inborn. It is in us, our everyday of our life. Only that we do not realise it. Life-radiance has been buried beneath us waiting to be discovered. The very moment we experience life-loving and life-giving, we will instantly experience life-radiance.

However, there is also a catch. Be careful and alert. At times when you smile at others there may be some words from the other that you may be out of your mind or you have some ulterior motive. You need then to be very cautious especially from the male species to smile at the opposite sex from a man to a lady.

There are times also, you will experience cold shoulder from the other party without even flinching or look at you when you smile. You can be gracious, always smiling. I was told by some parents with young children. Whenever, a child wants something, he or she would smile readily to his or her parent. That innocent smile, that radiant smile would put a parent off with light-heartedness. The parent would notice that the child wants something that may not be good for him or her. So be on your toes when you smile, be ever ready that there may not be any reciprocal from the other party,

For family members, especially when there is a disagreement or argument between spouses or children, someone has to take the lead to be ready to bring out that radiant smile, either by acknowledging the mistakes, to forgive the other or to make amends and reconcile. That someone is you.

One story if you have read or know about, it was short stories compiled by Leo Tolstoy that was read by many ardent readers. It was about an Emperor, long ago, seeking a philosophy of life. He needed wisdom to guide his rule and to govern by him. Other religions and philosophies during his reign did not satisfy him at all. Eventually he realised that in life the answers to only three fundamentals questions which needed to be answered by anyone. The three questions were:-

1. *When is the most important time?*
2. *Who is the most important person?*
3. *What is the most important thing to do?*

The emperor found his answers when he visited a hermit in the mountains. The questions mention is for you to reflect upon. I am very certain by taking your time to answer them will help you to be more confident in life and be more alert doing things you like to do. Do not rush to answer them. Take a minute or two to reflect before reading on.

When is the most important time? It is **NOW.** It is for all of us to have and hold that radiance in our life. That is the only time we ever have right now. So if we were to hold our loved ones so dear, our parents in expressing the love to them, how grateful you are for them, do it now. Give them a smile so cheerful and then hug them so tenderly. Cry if you must. It is a healing process. It is love. It is life-loving, life-giving and life-radiance all in one. It is for us now to uphold this radiance to smile at others no matter who they are. They can be man on the streets, your colleagues, your loved ones or even the helpless, the poor. Communication and love can only be shared when the one you are with, no matter who they are, is the most important person for you.

What about the most important person? Who is that person? Try to think and imagine who that person can be. It is **YOU**. You are the most important person in your own way of life. If you have said your parents, your spouse, your friends you can be right too. But **YOU** come first. You need to have that life-radiance in you before you could say your parents, your spouse, friends to be the most important people.

Next, what is the most important thing to do? Well, here you need to know very well – to care, to smile and bring on that cheerfulness in you if you have not started at all. It is not too late to do so, to **SMILE**. It is through smile and to care brings together in being careful and caring. We can show our caring attitude to others. However, being careful is an issue that we should learn to know how to care, how to be careful less others might take advantage of us, being too over-careful that we can be conned by others.

Maitri (pronounce as My Tree) is loving-kindness, friendliness, benevolence, amity, friendship, goodwill, kindness and active interest in other.. And we can let it be what it is without giving ourselves a hard time, which is the quality of maitri. Thus maitri itself is really more of an attitude, more of an experience, a softness and gentleness in our experience. It is a nonjudgementalness attitude to all aspects of our experience. How to apply maitri? It is simply to acknowledge ourselves by having that life-radiance in us. By having experience life-radiance, we can also acknowledge to acquire life-loving and life-giving too. Being able to make good and helpful choices depends on freeing ourselves from self-aggression. We can then begin to start developing maitri ourselves and then it naturally extend our as compassion toward others.

In the Scriptures of Ecclesaistes, the words speak very clear to us. Some of them are real meaning to know about what we need to go through in our life. It said: "There is a time for everything, and a season for every activity. This first sentence opens up to let us know that there is always time for us to activate ourselves in acknowledging what we should do and shouldn't do.

Just to share my experience whenever I take the public transport or walk around on the streets. Out of twenty persons, almost all of them would be holding their cell phone. These people will use their cell phones either by texting messages, reading them, playing some online games or watching a movie. Some even have I-pad or laptops. As I looked around, I was aware that those who use the cell phones, after a few minutes they doze off. Parents would spoil their children in order to get an I-pad or cell phone for them. Their intention was to keep their children quiet and busy. At food court, while waiting for food one can notice that at every table at least five persons will use cell phone texting away. This kind of technology has made many us being too individualistic. Individualism has conquered mankind. Technology has also conquered mankind. Although it is good that we have such high technology communication with easy contact with our friends, loved ones and family members, we need to understand that such technology should be used for a good cause and not to allow technology take control of our lives. We do not care about others. We only concentrate on ourselves. Even crossing the road, you will notice that pedestrian will text messages while crossing the road. Where is that life-radiance?

It seems that all the life-loving, life-giving and life-radiance just disappear without everyone notices. It would be exercise for you. Try to take the public transport, the bus or the train, watch and look around you, how many can you count to know people only concentrate on themselves in texting messages, watching movies or playing online games. I may be one of the guilty one too.

But it is not too late. I realise that this is not the life style we are in. Thus I will always look around me in the buses, trains or even on the streets looking at all the people doing their own things. They do not care what happen in front of them. Will they be alert if there is an earthquake or a building collapses? Why can't we enjoy the journey look around the environment, appreciate the landscape, the building structures etc. instead of just paying attention to oneself. Of course there are people dozing off too. It is normal for them perhaps they are tired out and had not enough sleep the previous day or night.

Life-radiance is meant for all of us. It is as though an in-born for us to acknowledge this. But we at times fail to do so. That's why we have so many problems in terms of war, fights political issues in the world. Nations against nations, country against country, people against people and even in the household, family against one another, spouse against one another or even children against one another. There seems to be no peace at all.

It is not too late to adhere and understand the meaning of life-radiance. Cultivate and nurture life-radiance in you. By doing so, we will be at peace with ourselves first then with others around us. Maitri is the very type for us to instil in us the friendship, the kindness, benevolence and the very nature of maitri teachings in our life. Why not do it now? Why wait till we are aging? We can start from the very young. Do it now before it is too late when we die and we don't see eye to eye as what in the Living Years lyrics mention.

Our life is about doing things having our own, leading only to our own world. Love is an enduring one, it needs to be fed with emotions, with empathy with care. Love also needs to be created for a purpose to be alive on this earth. We are to portray ourselves with loving others. The more you serve others, the more fulfilled your life will be. Albert Einstein closed it very aptly that the highest destiny of the individual is to serve. To turn our backs on a life of service is to turn our backs on our very selves. Service is at the very core of our identity as human beings.

Isn't this very true? If you were to notice around you, on the streets, in the bus, in the train or anywhere, people today are unconsciously promoting self-centredness that paralyzes the human spirit.

Now is the time. There will never a better time to begin with your self-radiance that is to smile and greet people around, your folks, your co-workers, your neighbours. Thus the very first step to take to becoming perfectly yourself is acknowledging your imperfections. No one is perfect. We are created to be born into this world with imperfections. The only thing that you can do is to be yourself.

No one has demonstrated that more than Victor Frankl did in Man's Search for Meaning as he recalled his experiences in Nazi concentration camps during World War II. Over and over, he encountered people who even though they were starving would share their inadequate rations with others. Victor Frankl explained that while some were killing themselves or wallowing in self-pity, others were filled with an inexplicable happiness, a real joy that was independent of substance or circumstances. It was what exactly in life-radiance which means we share our joy, our happiness with others. Victor Frankl truly explained in his own words of being happy no matter how difficult life is. By having the life-radiance in you, you are able to bring about that happiness to others. Life is about love, What do you love doing? Do it. What do you love being? Be it. What do you love having? Have it and share it. Who do you love loving? Love them. These are the exact words written by Matthew Kelly in his book of Perfectly Yourself of nine lessons for enduring happiness.

So do open the door of your heart. This is by trying to be hospitable. If we have that kind of hospitality opening the doors to our hearts, we are inviting people to connect us in our daily lives. We never know what we may be inviting or rather encounter when we let others know that we are available and ready to help. If we help we get much more than we may have bargained for. Having that self-radiance, we can always be ready and willing to be there for someone who is in need. Perhaps by having that listening ear telling that someone, 'hey I am here for you'. How can I help you?

Of course, you need to be cautious when someone approaches you seeking help. If possible to assist in what way you can. If you can't then be truthful about it because at times that someone may be in financial distress and you are unable to help. Give advice, be there, show empathy, be compassionate, you can't solve the problem for him or her. Try to have that kind of smiling positive attitude which means create in you that self-radiance.

Every morning I take the bus to work from my home. That is one particular bus captain who is so polite in greeting commuters when they board his bus. He would say 'good morning', 'come on up', 'be careful', 'hold on tight'. It has really made my day. So whenever I board the bus and he is the bus captain as I can recognize him easily, I would reciprocate and return the greeting. However, there are some commuters, perhaps they got up on the wrong side of the bed, grouchy, not enough sleep the previous night. These do not return the greeting at all, simply ignore him. Yet he takes in every stride, doesn't matter as long he does the greeting and that is enough for him. I am very amazed about him. This is what we should do. No matter what, if others do not return the greeting or the smile, never mind. As long as you have done it which will make your day, be happy with that life-radiance.

The following chapter is life-upheaval. It is matter of having the upheavals in our lives. Why? Without having the life-loving, life-giving and life-radiance, we at times will have the life-upheavals in us. Even if we do not practice the mentioned virtues, we may also have experience upheavals.

Life-Upheaval

What is the meaning of upheaval? It is a major change of period of change that causes a lot of conflict, confusion, anger, etc.

Some of us have experienced major upheavals in early life or later stage of life or even ongoing experience. Life-upheaval is a kind of life that we should try not to be in the stage of upheaval. I know one person – a lady who lost her husband to cancer. It was a stage that when the husband, James had some coughing problem that has made him somewhat rather weak whenever he coughed. He could cough so badly that he at times could not sleep or even wake up early for work. His wife Jessie advised him to see a doctor. He refused thinking that perhaps, the pain might go away in a few days. Well, the pain did not subside. Eventually he went for a medical check-up. Result came out that he had lung cancer in the third stage. This had made them more worried as James was a sole breadwinner supporting Jessie and their four school going children. Jessie tried to find employment but due to her age if she reached 40 years old, it was not easy. She wanted to help supplement the income in case James could not work or even would be asked to stop work from his employer.

This made them more worried and every day they are thinking of their financial problem. It was a major upheaval for them. Thus the upheaval had made them to be more stressful always thinking of the future. James and Jessie hardly had a good night sleep since he was diagnosed with the disease. It had never to them for their 15 years of marriage. Jessie was worried of what to do if James were to leave them as so early an age of 39. Jessie was only 36 years old. How was she going to manage the family without the father figure at home. It seemed she had to learn how to be a father and a mother to her children. When major life events happen to us, we can only see what's right in front of us; we can't see the far-reaching consequences around the bend, the good that can come of tragedy. It would not be easy for people like James and Jessie or even to anyone of us when tragedy strikes. When such upheaval occurs as what we can imagine is the life-upheaval, we need to take stock of the future of what we really want in our life.

Are we prepared for anything, come what may? Are we really prepared for this kind of journey to experience life-upheaval? I believe that all of us have such experience in our life. It has to happen. We cannot avoid this upheaval thingy. We need to think and be alert when things occur in our life, our work, our marriage, in our home, our children, our friends and co-workers.

Bernard shared his story about his brother Timothy who had lung cancer.

"He had bad cough and tire easily whenever he went out. Even walking a few steps, he became breathless. He went for a medical check-up and diagnosed by doctors that his cancer was in the third stage. All of us were shocked and could not believe that Timothy was ill."

"Subsequently, he became terminally ill that he needed to be admitted to hospice care. He was in pain and often requested for painkiller drugs. We spent endless days with him to be with him at the last moment. As I remembered before he was admitted, he requested me to pray for him for healing. Well, I did, but told him to have faith. He refused to believe this saying he had young children with him and not willing to let go to die. I felt helpless, what could I do to give him comfort.

He had sleepless nights. We tried as much to ease him but in vain. The only way I did was to pray the **"Three Beautiful Prayers".** This prayer was recited by a curate named John in Rome. It had since been made known all over the world. This prayer is useful to a dying person that he or she will accept his or her fate of the remaining days on earth. Well, I believed so, recited the prayers and guess what. Timothy slept peacefully for three days. We had good rest. However, after the third day he woke up. Few hours later, he breathed his last. It was in the month of June 1994. Ten years later after my father's death in the same month.

"It was really life-upheaval for us," Bernard said, "it was especially so for mother and us, his wife and children. Mother was hysterically, remembering that father passed away in the same month. For us too to bring back that memory of death. Why? After ten years. It had to be an answer, but God only knows. This life-upheaval, all of us have to accept no matter what, it has to be so for us."

I know of some couples who have gone through such situation. One very good example when a couple, both are divorcee and they met one another at some functions, they started to click and get along. Now the problem is this. One partner wanted to know the other partner whereabouts. Paul met Pauline during an event. They introduced themselves. They began dating for about two years. Everything was so blissful, planning for second marriage, starting a home etc. Then came this 'where you go' 'what you do' who you went out with whom' – so many questions, well Pauline couldn't take it when Paul kept on questioning her about her rendezvous. They split up go their own way. Somehow, Paul couldn't take it and kept on harping about their relationship. Paul was adamant wanting to hit off and carry on. Pauline was unsure about such relationship. They needed to solve the problem between themselves. To them this life-upheaval had taken a toll of their matured life. Paul was afraid to go through such life as he was divorced and left his matrimonial by not being able to see eye to eye with his wife. He has a daughter whom he dotes on her. Pauline seems to like Paul's daughter who has taken a liking with Pauline. When his daughter Clare knew about the split, she was heartbroken. She hopes that her father and Pauline could get back together. I discussed with them, giving them some thoughts to think about how they should or shouldn't get back together.

Eventually they get on well, but how long it would be, we cannot know the future. Life-upheaval is a life that we cannot see in the future. We only need now is to enjoy every moment of our life to be better people, better character to be sure that life-upheaval is a life to be of harmony and calm and not upheaval of storms to blow us apart.

Paul seemed to be very accommodating to Pauline. Pauline seemed to understand Paul better now knowing about his character and behaviour. Thus each of them has decided to move on, taking life-upheaval with them as long as they live making very sure that life-upheaval would be only peace and love for one another. As I said, how long will the relationship last? We really do not know the future. It is left to be seen. However, it is also our part, their part to be accommodating to one another.

Viktor Frankl in his writing of "Man's Searching for Meaning", in view of the possibility of finding meaning in suffering, life's meaning is an unconditional one, at least potentially. He said that just as life remains potentially meaningful under any conditions, even those which are most miserable, so too does the value of each and every person stay with him or her. It does so because it is based on the values that he or she has realized in the past, and is not contingent on the usefulness that he or she may or may not retain in the present. It is only right, dear reader, that as we go through life-upheaval, we need to know and understand our own suffering and also of others. There are those who have gone through more hardships in suffering than you can imagine. Your suffering may be only on tip of the iceberg. If we have this experience, we can then understand and empathise those who have the similar kind of suffering in the upheaval situation.

Everything in life, no matter what situation you are in, it is about how you feel. The decision you make in your life is also based on how you feel. It is in your own motivating factor of your entire life is your own feelings. So what Gautama Buddha in his teachings said: ***"Holding on to anger is like grasping a hot coal with the intent of throwing it at someone else; you are the one getting burned."***

For negativity attitude, all the negative words such as blame, criticism, finding fault and even complaining about others are just mere words that can hurt others whenever these are spoken out. Thus, in being positive, life-upheaval is just the lifestyle we are going through today. In trying to love others, you can have whatever you love and want, but you need seriously think of harmonizing with love.

> *"All that we send into the lives of others*
> *comes back into our own."*
> *(Edwin Markham 1852-1940), Poet*

It is important for us to note that we recognize the progress we make in our lives. Our family, our loved ones, our friends, our heritage are important to have a better and fulfilling life. It's positive reinforcement. It is one of the most crucial ingredients in leading a happy, fulfilled life.

William James, one of the brilliant philosophers ever lived declared: "The greatest discovery in our generation is that human beings, by changing the inner attitudes of their minds can change the outer aspects of their lives." So what does attitude mean and does it do? It is like this, when anything happens in our lives, the message or stimulus comes through our senses into our minds and then one of our attitudes interprets, evaluates and pronounces judgment. We tend to be judgmental towards others not thinking about them, but thinking of ourselves only. We are all guilty of such attitude behaviour. I am also guilty too of such behaviour. It tends to react in anger, frustration and easy flaring up. It happens to me at my workplace when was given a task to do. I was trying my best to perform. Sometimes, co-workers feel they are not appreciated in their work. Thus, our life-upheaval too occurs in workplace which at times can create a conflict among co-workers. All of us are trying our best to excel in career, in financial situation, but when things go wrong, we intend to blame others but not ourselves. We tend to say those around us cause the upheavals in our lives.

All of us have our weaknesses. We tend to hide ourselves in closets, covering our weak points in our lives. Life-upheaval is like that. We tend to cover up ourselves thinking that this shouldn't happen to us but let it happen to others. We have to experience upheavals in our lives so that we can grow to be better people, character change and better behaviour. John Powell also said that most of us find hard to live with others. We're all so different that it's difficult to put any two people together without getting some kind of disagreement or conflict. We have that guilt in us. We are thinking only of ourselves, thus creating the life-upheavals ourselves and not for others. We are the creator of upheavals. So who is to blame who? Anyone we can blame? No, we are to blame ourselves for this upheaval creation.

Can we remember the goodness in us? That goodness surfaced and showed through when we responded to love. If you are like others how the hurt and defensive self-surfaces and shone through when you were criticized and attacked. Can you remember any of such episodes in your life? When we think about it, actually it is doing to ourselves, this hurt and defensive attitude. We assume the role of the critic. We need to change that kind of attitude. Be a friend to ourselves. Love ourselves. Although there will be upheavals still, but we can have that contained and not to create more upheavals. It will definitely make a big difference in our lives.

Psychiatrist Victor Frankl has said that it would be wiser to let life question us. When we look at the stars or a garden, for instance, life is asking. "Can you appreciate beauty?" When someone in pain or troubles comes into our lives, it asks, "Are you capable of sympathy?" At other times, life simply asks, "Do you ever allow yourself to enjoy?" Life will ask, "What do you want from me?" We have all the different answers. Some of us may say about survival. As long I survive, I am ok. Why should I care about others?

Let them have their own way, let them lead their own life. Most of us will have such thoughts.

But I said to you when having developed a positive self-feeding cycle in your life, you will be able to achieve anything if you put your mind to it. So are you preparing to have life-fulfilment? If you do so, people will notice the change in your attitude and outlook. By noticing your change, they will begin to change theirs as well.

> **"The person who lives life fully, glowing with life's energy, is the person who lives a successful life." – Daisaku Ikeda**

So even if you have not started to understand life fully without knowing about life-upheavals, it is not too late to start and have that decision to know more of what life is all about. Life is not only in living with money, not being rich or poor, not being homeless, or even getting at one another's nerve like I must win and you must lose. No, life is not like that. Life is more than that. It is to open up your heart, your very being to accept others no matter who they are, whether poor, rich homeless, living in tatters, without family members, without parents.

It is what Maria Robinson author of The Journey's End once said, "*Nobody can go back and start a new beginning, but anyone can start today and make a new ending.*" Nothing could be closer to the truth. But before you can begin this process of transformation you have to stop doing the things that have been holding you back.

If someone wants you in their life, they'll make room for you. It is the person who stand beside you when you're at your worst, down and out they are your true friends and it's not the people who stand by your side when you're at your best.

Howard Falco writing in his book of 'I AM', it said resistance is the force that is at the heart of all the energy of the universe. Without it there would be no world of relativity and no universe in which to experience life. Again what Howard Falco mentioned is the transformation to a new person – **YOU** that has already begun. You become aware of what you are, how you created your past and why you have held yourself back from receiving the answers that would lead you to experience a new future, you become more aware of the potential of who and what you can be. It is this, to love and accept yourself just as you are and who you are in order to understand the life-upheavals that have been in us ever since the creation of mankind.

> *"Your life does not get better by chance,*
> *it gets better by change."*
> **-Jim Rohn**
> **Author and Motivational Speaker,**
> **September 1930 to December 2009**

Look at it this way. Life-upheaval can also mean things to happen in our daily lives. Take for example the incidents of a disappearance of an airplane or airplane crashed with passengers on board. Thus if this had to happen, it is a mystery. Why should this happen? What is the reason behind such incidents? How about those surviving families knowing the loss of their family members? It has to happen to all of us in such life-upheaval. When this happen, can we take it? Some will suffer shocks, some will go into depression knowing that their loved ones were dead.

Well, life-upheaval is just there for all of us. No matter where we are, no matter what we do, if we do not realise about life-upheaval. It is a matter of time, if we really prepare ourselves when we can to understand this life-upheaval. It is to stay in our life, if we know how to handle life-upheaval. We need strength. We need consolation. We need comfort. So dear reader, do give yourself a thought about life-upheaval. Do what we can to help others in terms of opening our hearts, our hands to those in need. Those who are in need not really in monetary terms, but perhaps in terms of comfort when there is stress, where is distress, where there is discomfort or when someone lost the loved one.

> *"What lies behind us*
> *And what lies before us*
> *Are tiny matters*
> *Compared to what lies within us."*
>
> *-Anonymous*
> -

I find this quotation very true. We do not know what lies behind us or even ahead of us. What lies within us is more important if we know what to deal with life-upheaval.

We feel in life-upheaval we cannot let go of the past. If we can learn to let go, we can learn to understand that time is short. If someone asks you for help than that's something you can do not as you choose. You cannot bring back the past as there is nothing we can do about it. Past is past, look forward to the future. You must turn your attention to the here and now.

Isn't this very true? Most of us will always look back of the past. Most of us will pinpoint the problems of the past to the person – loved ones or even our closest friend. Such comments – "Last year you promise me to get things for me. You always blame me for things I did not do. You don't respect me. You make me feel embarrass always comparing those who are better than me."

There are many kinds of such comments. We do not seem to give compliments to others. We hardly say thank you to others when things went right.

Life-Fulfilment

What is life-fulfilment? There are many versions of the meaning of the word fulfilment. What does a fulfilling or fulfilled life mean to us? Everyone has his or her own definition of a fulfilling or fulfilled life.

Oprah Winfrey's quotation said that **"real success means creating a life of meaning through service that fulfils your reason for being here."**

"It is not in the pursuit of happiness that we find fulfilment, it is in the happiness of pursuit." - Denis Waitley.

Confucius also said that – **"The will to win, the desire to succeed, the urge to reach your full potential…these are the keys that will unlock the door to personal excellence."**

So, what do you think about life-fulfilment. I'm wondering about the word fulfilment, what counts as a fulfilled life. Is it success (career)? Is it happiness or full of love? It is to have fun in life because life doesn't last forever. So what is your own definition of living a life so fulfilled?

"Occasionally in life there are those moments of unutterable fulfilment which cannot be completely explained by those symbols called words. Their meanings can only be articulated by the inaudible language of the heart."
-Martin Luther King Jr.

-

When someone says that he or she have lived life to the fullest, it doesn't really mean that he or she have climbed the highest mountain in the world or grew old with age to live with the one whom he or she loved. Life-fulfilment means that is to me, that someone has found peace in his life. If that is you, you have all that you desired which really comes to is personal opinion. Whatever you perceive within yourself that you have lived out your entire life, than it is, I dare say you have found fulfilment in your life without any regrets.

At times, we live with regrets. We, say for example have found someone to marry and live together, spending time together, loving each other throughout the marriage life. Then after some years later, through some hardships, intolerance, one spouse will say – why I marry him or her? What is the point? Have I lived a fulfilled life? I can't take it anymore. That's it. Enough is enough. Hey, hold on, hold your horses! You have made the vows you have cherished the moments together. What about the good memories spending time together? Children! Where do they come from? They are the image of both of you. They are the creation of yourselves. Life-fulfilled! I should say yes. The only reason is that both parties don't see eye to eye at the situation. We have to go through ups and downs in life. Without problems, without situations, life is meaningless. Life is so colourless. Life is not life at all. Life has no goals at all. Life is short. Anytime, one spouse will die and leaving behind the other one. Everything in life is meant to change. So learn to let go and go on the journey together living together. I do have setbacks in my family. I do have upheavals in some circumstances. I have tried and will always try to be tolerant in the family. I know that life is short. I want to enjoy life as it is to have a more meaningful life, to fulfil life, enjoying every moment of it whether it is working, leisure, relaxation or going away for holiday to be stress free without anxiety at all. I want to make myself to experience the fulfilment of life.

We do at times have anxiety disorder. But if we know we have, there is a need not to be too overly anxious in every little things, worrying, having sleepless nights, waking at every moment, thinking of all the things undone during the day or preparing for the next day worrying whether the next day would go well. No point! Useless, we will suffer in future, we will have depression, having the anxiety disorder that will bring us down, that we cannot bring ourselves up and standing on our own two feet.

Most of us have the tendency to take life for granted. We think that what we have now, it is a life-fulfilled. No, I disagree to this. Our life-fulfilled is a life that we have to carry on living without regrets. We live on this earth – it is just a journey, a temporary home to live life to the fullest. However, mankind to this day has become so selfish that most of us think we do really live a life with fulfilment.

Life-fulfilling is to have that exuberance in us, that kind of emotions to understand others, putting others before us. It is a service to others not in terms of monetary values, but in time, in offering service to help those unfortunate. As mentioned in the earlier chapter I for one am always ready to experience the fulfilment of life by volunteering myself to community work.

"Our greatness lies not so much in being able to remake the world as being able to remake ourselves." - Mahatma Gandhi

At times some of us will view the sources of happiness and fulfilment in each other's life. Some of us may experience some good days and bad days. No matter what the experience is, we must still strive to make us feel better and enjoy each day as it is. Life-fulfillment is not meant to just ok I give up and I don't think I can achieve anything, nothing has been fulfilled at all.

I have experiences some bad days at times in constant state of doubt and disarray. I have been searching, wondering when the next positive experience would come along so that I could feel good again. At times, I could feel some destructive days, some days could make me just to give up and surrendering to my dead self as I can't do anything right. But, I realise that if I give up, I will suffer more and be downtrodden, no one will pick me up when I fall into despair.

So dear reader, try to be aware of your mindset, feelings and emotions. By doing so, you can work toward finding peace of mind. You can then conquer fear, doubt and not be so negative towards life. I will agree with you that it is easier said than done. Yes, hard times will fall upon us all. Emotions tend to get haywire from time to time. However, by accepting what come your way is to commit to the changing view how to deal with the troubles encountered and this will make a real difference in your life. Nobody can make it happen – ONLY YOU. Thus in order for your life to change for the better, you have to change first. Feeling happy and content became a choice rather than an occurrence. This is how I feel to be contented is a choice.

To live a life of fulfilment, to be realistic and happy is to change for the better. We can if we want to change our lifestyle. It is upon ourselves to do and no one else can help in change our lifestyle to modify our behaviour. We need to have that social graciousness, be responsible and live courageously. How we fulfil our life is all up to us.

No one else can tell us how to enjoy life and make it more fulfilling. Living a fulfilled life can be very enriching. It depends how we look at different perspective. Some may look at a life fulfilling to be provider at home and work all their lives. While others may enjoy life to the fullest to really take things in a stride that do not put them down and feel depressed. There are others who look life in a different way to make things better such as enjoying what they like to do like hobby, sight-seeing, taking things easy, more relax, no boredom or even be volunteer to help others who are in dire needs of emotional support or material needs.

I know there are others who do not enjoy life at all. They find life so meaningless, so unfulfilling. One couple I know said that they have to work all their lives to support the family. Without work, they are unable to enjoy life as they need to fulfil some financial needs to support themselves and their children. Although they find life so boring, they still need to work hard.

Life-Journey

In this chapter of life-journey, life is a journey. It is filled with many setbacks, many good things, with celebrations. The journey we undertake will never be smooth sailing. The road will not always be smooth. In fact, during the travelling on this earth, we will face many challenges. Are we prepared to accept such challenges? Along the way we may stumble upon, we may fall, facing many obstacles as we go on this life-journey. How strong are we in this journey of life? Sometimes when we face many challenges and upheavals, we do not realise that such challenges can be a blessing for us. When we encounter these setbacks, we begin to feel disgruntle, we begin to feel disappointed, depressed and all the other problems we face. It is our choice. We will have people giving us advice on how to live a life, how to go on a journey in our life. Ultimately, we have our own choice of how to live and what we feel is right. At times, we think that we are right in living our life, but others from the outside will notice that we are not living rightly at all. Thus, we need our loved ones, our close friends to tell us about living a life so blissful, so happening in joys and celebrations.

When will our journey end on this earth? We may never know. We are travellers on this earth. It is only a temporary shelter, temporary accommodation. We strive to live to gain experience in life. Our journey will end only when the time is ripe for us to leave this earth. In accidents, no matter where we are- on the road, at home, anything can happen, through illness.. So how much have we done for ourselves to gain happiness, to gain life and be contented what we have? We tend to complain, tend to be envious of others who have more than us. We want to challenge and be better people than others. We become so proud of ourselves to take the opportunity to climb higher and higher to gain popularity. Then one day, we will fall flat to the ground. We feel miserable because of our failures.

I was inspired with the title – "**Life Is Like A Cup Of Coffee**". It is from an unknown author. Look up at Youtube of the same title.

Here it is for me to share with you.

A group of alumni, highly established in their careers, got together to visit their old university professor. Conversation soon turned into complaints about stress in work and life.

Offering his guests coffee, the professor went to the kitchen and returned with a large pot of coffee and an assortment of cups – porcelain, plastic, glass, crystal, some plain looking, some expensive, some exquisite – telling them to help themselves to the coffee.

When all the students had a cup of coffee in hand, the professor said: "If you noticed, all the nice looking expensive cups have been taken up, leaving behind the plain and cheap ones. While it is normal for you to want only the best for yourselves, that is the source of your problems and stress.

Be assured that the cup itself adds no quality to the coffee. In most cases it is just more expensive and in some cases even hides what we drink. What all of you really wanted was coffee, not the cup, but you consciously went for the best cups. And then you began eyeing each other's cups.

Now consider this: Life is the coffee; the jobs, money and position in society are the cups. They are just tools to hold and contain Life, and the type of cup we have does not define, nor change the quality of life we live.

Sometimes, by concentrating only on the cup, we fail to enjoy the coffee. Savor the coffee, not the cups! The happiest people don't have the best of everything. They just make the best of everything. Live simply. Love generously. Care deeply. Speak kindly.

Dear reader, you get what the above really mean? It is in our life-journey, we do not know when we will leave this earth. Life is really short. What the unknown author said is for us to savor the coffee not the cups. It is very important for us to understand the true meaning of life. How we live, how we get along with others, it is our choice to make. We can't blame anyone turmoil of life that invades us, spoiling our lives to make us feel we do not care for others at all.

Our life journey, when will it end? We really don't at all. So are we prepared that one day we may not be here today but gone forever? Thus life is a journey here on earth. We live on earth is just a temporary shelter, temporary home.

We cannot live a life full of roses. There are thorns in our life. It is a journey filled with lessons, hardships, heartaches, joys, celebrations and special moments that will ultimately led us to our destination, our purpose in life. The road will not always be smooth, in fact throughout our travels, we will encounter many challenges. It is really true that as we journey in our life, we face many obstacles. Along our journey we will be confronted with many situations, some will be filled with joy and some will be filled with heartaches. How we react to what we are faced with determines what kind of outcome the rest of our journey through life will be like. Well, some of the challenges we will be tested for our courage, strengths, weaknesses and faith. To be on the right path, we must overcome these obstacles. At times, these obstacles are meant for us as blessings, only we do not realize this at that time.

Life is full of inconveniences. There will always be interruptions and difficult people around us. We can't control all our circumstances, but we can control our reactions. Too many people these days have the wrong approach to life. They think they can't be happy unless they control all their circumstances and everything goes their way.

So what is life about? Is life a journey? But a journey to where exactly?

Life-Reasoning

What does the word Reason mean? It is the capacity for consciously making sense of things, applying logic, verify facts and beliefs based on new or existing information. Reasoning is associated with thinking, cognition and intellect.

Cognitive scientists and psychologists have attempted to study and explain how people reason. Example as such it is on which cognitive and neural processes are engaged and how cultural factors affect the inferences that people draw.

Western literature often treated reason as being opposed to emotions and feelings. This was an understanding of human nature developed. You might say that passions made you behave contrary to reason or that your reason kept the passion under control. Thus it is expressed colloquially as the dilemma between following "the head" - reason or "the heart" – emotions.

We reason and act the way that we do strictly in response to the environment in which we find ourselves. How is it so? It is because most of the time given to our socialization into some cultural factors, certain situations prompt us to act in anticipated and predictable way. Culture sets norms for how we behave as members of the families, friends, colleagues at workplace and our neighbours.

We have the obligation to understand about life reasoning. It is when we were brought into this world, it is for a reason. The reason is to live life not only for ourselves but for others too. We need to know the reason why some people behave in awkward situations and some are able to have the comprehension in knowing the real reason in being alive until the day we will face our Creator.

It is not an easy task for us if we do fail to appreciate life and knowing its reason for the world. If we take one step at a time, seeking the real reason to be on this earth, we will then appreciate the many things life has given us. But how many of us do appreciate it? We tend to behave for each man for himself. You would say, as long as I am ok and can live life without any reason to help others, we feel we can live longer and grow old gracefully. Well, it may not be so.

As Scriptures say, do unto others as you would like them do unto you. It simply means that if we can tolerate each other and knowing its reason of the behaviour, we will then say to ourselves that our friends, neighbours, colleagues need help to know the reason of living and surviving.

The evidence suggests strongly that we can identify with persons unknown to us. It is also about care of what is happening to them. It is our primary and deep relationships to help others. Such reasoning prompts and shapes in helping in determining moral action.

Life reasoning will always be in us, if we know how to really seek with wisdom knowing the meaning behind it. We need to be alert in finding ways of why some people behave in such manner that affects society at large and others find it irritating and frustrating. Knowing such bad attitude of people, we tend to be biased and even give reasons that they are not fit to be in the society with you. We will find ways to reason out that we are better than this awkward behaviour of some characters.

Life reasoning is not to be this way. It is to have a better life and better living to succeed. We are meant to succeed in certain ways and not to be too competitive of each other.

Some of us will reason out and then be envious of others who are successful in their lives. We reason ourselves that we are hopeless, useless and uncompetitive. In this way, we will never be able to prove ourselves of living a life that we should live for ourselves.

More often than not, we tend to find ways of reasoning with others especially with our loved ones at home. We tend to make assumptions that our loved ones have to give reasons why they behave in certain manner. We tend to argue about in reaching to a point that we are better than the other if they do not give any reasons of their behaviour. For example, if a teenager wanted to go out for a date and without giving any reason to the parent, not telling the parent of the intended date, the parent would surely want to know its reason for the date and with whom the teenager is going out with. Thus without giving reason, the parent would then refuse the teenager to go out on a date. When reason not given, quarrels would ensue and there will be disagreement. If a parent and the teenager are close and loving, definitely the teenager would give reason saying that it is just a friendly date with others in the group.

Another thing for life reasoning is the trust for each other. Without trust, there is no purpose of reasoning. Trust is also important and with reason, the world will be a better place to live in.

I truly believe that we need to live and have a life reasoning attitude and behaviour towards others and not to abandon those who do not know the true meaning of reasoning in their lives. When we do unto others, we will expect them to do unto us.

When we came into this world, we were born helpless. We are entirely dependent of others. Our finitude is a constitutive feature of who we are and what we are. We could no longer survive socially if we behave in asocial or unsocial ways. In humanness, human beings are very complex, very confusing and indecisive at times or maybe almost every time. In such life reasoning, we should meet everyone in our life. By meeting people along our path, everything that may happen there is a reason for it to happen. It brings us lessons to learn which are important. By understanding such incidents, we tend to become grateful for everyone and everything that has happened. In so doing, we will begin to see life in a different way. Thus for reasoning, we make decision when something happens. When we make different decisions, something different will happen. It is in reasoning there are choices of decision. Either we choose, no matter whatever decision we make, there is bound to happen for something else in terms of wrong decision make. At times the outcome can be awful or beautiful when making right decision.

Life-Controlling

What is the purpose of life? What is the meaning of life when it involves life controlling issues? There are some of us who feel we need to be the controlling factor – to control our loved ones, our spouse, our partner and friends. They feel that by controlling they will be great and people will look up to them. This is not true at all. It is what some will say they are the control freak people. By controlling other people's lives in the way they want them to behave and listen to the control freak, it is not life at all. A wise saying, that you will never be happy if you continue to search for what happiness consist of in controlling others, you will never live if you are looking for the meaning of life the way you want to live in by taking control. It is better to be proactive by educating yourself about control issues so that you will have a better perspective of how to improve your relationship. Life is for us live and not to be controlled by others. Life is freedom for all of us to live happily and be contented, to be thankful. It is better to spend time exploring the controlling issues that lead to anger and resentment in the interactions with your family members, loved ones and friends or even your colleagues. Listen more than you talk. Learn to understand that someone next to you of what he or she thinks or what he or she is going to say.

Are there people who like to be in control of others? Yes, I should think so. It is either the male or female partner, one of them like to control the other. A case I recently heard not too long ago. It was about a couple who were in relationship for two years or so. Both parties are divorced. They met when they went on a group date. The man is the one who controlled the lady. Every time, the lady went out with her friends, the man insisted of knowing where she went and whom she went out with. She must be at his beck and call. She must seek his permission whether she can go out with her group of friends. For whatever reason, she must let him know the purpose of her outing. The man seems to feel insecure and paranoid that he may lose her to other men. This problem took off for sometimes until the lady could not take it anymore and they decided to go on their own way. It seems she is much happier to be on her own and with her own life that no one can control her. She can do what she wants without seeking permission at all.

Do we control people's life? Can the controlling factor make us happy to live a life so fulfilling? Is in our genes that this controlling attitude can take hold of us? We need to change, to understand the real situation before we can take control of others. It is so much easier to blame your partner than to look at yourself and this especially true when relationship control issues are involved.

Whatever your role in the relationship either too controlling or too passive there are steps to start your relationship with anyone, be it your loved ones, at home or even in your working place as colleagues. Do not let yourself be a control freak. The steps to take not allowing yourself be that control freak, is to focus on becoming more self- aware of your own behaviour. Take full responsibility for yourself either it being too controlling or being too passive. There are some instances for either spouse or parents to be control freaks. When a wife is the controlling factor, her husband has to make way to be the victim of the control. This is unhealthy. Both parties must understand one another better so that the controlling character in either party would not exist at all. Believe that change is possible for both parties not allowing the controlling image be there. We need to understand one another. We need to love and be forgiving and be slow to anger.

We need to be rich in kindness and at the same time be rich in love. All we need to do is to remember the goodness of God in our lives. So thus let us lead one another in terms of graciousness, kindness and love. Let no hatred be in our hearts and souls. Do not allow that character of a control freak be present in us.

Life controlling can be rather complex in our daily life. We tend to have split personality when we feel like to control others in the workplace, at home or in school. Children tend to misbehave, to be big bully to others like as though they are in charge of their school mates. I once did counsel a boy of 13 years old about three years ago. He studied in one of the most prestige school. He tends to take control of others in school, defying them that he was a better person and no one is better than him. Well, one of this classmate took the challenge and defied him. When I counselled him, he mentioned that his class mate requested he stole money from other students if he could prove that he can control others. This he did. He was caught stealing seen by other students. He was reprimanded. His parents were called in to discuss his behaviour. His mother could control him at home. It seemed that he bullied his sister at him whenever he had the chance to do so.. It seemed he was the mama's boy clinging to his mother all the time. When I met them, talked to him, he was so sheepish holding his mother's hand clinging to her. Mother did all the talking and answering questions put forward to him. He did purposefully not taking the lead to answer any questions put to him. What I did was to separate them, talk to him alone without his mother. He was rather quiet at first. He began to tell me about his behaviour in school. It seemed after number of times meeting them, he wanted was attention at home. I got his mother to reveal about the home environment. Attention was given fully to his younger sister all the time. His sister was somewhat mentally challenged. I visited them at home and discovered about this eventually. I told his parents that he needed some kind of attention and love from them. Well, his father was always busy working two jobs to make a living. His wife was unemployed taking of their daughter giving full attention to her needs. He had never been out with his father not even going down to shops together. I told them to give a try requesting the father to take the son out even perhaps a watch movie together. They did try but, somehow, the boy's behaviour had not change to be better. He was still rebellious, trying to control other people especially in his school. He was almost expelled from school, His mother pleaded with the principal requesting to give her son a second chance. In fact, at home he refused to study and do his homework. However with such behaviour, he came out tops in his school exams. The school was proud of him. It was amazing that he could excel in his study. After some years of meeting them, he began to change his behaviour the better. He moved on to his secondary level and became so studious. His parents were so proud of him. He went on for his exchange program overseas. The last time I heard of them was when he became so caring towards his sister.

Well, life controlling can be overcome, if there is someone who could be able to assist showing care and concern to the other party who is a control freak. If nothing has been done to repair the damage, life controlling in that person could be a lifetime and then it would be too late to manage and change that person.

At first if we know anyone who is a control freak, we should try to show empathy toward him or her. There must be some reason why this person's behaviour is such.

"Why do we get so hung up on what we do not agree on, when in fact it's our differences that make life interesting?"

– The Meaning of Life (Bradley Trevor Greive)

Life-Searching

"You will never be happy if you continue to search for what happiness consists of. You will never live if you are looking for the meaning of life."
-Albert Camus

Every one of us is always searching for the meaning of life. We search and search hoping to find what we want in terms of happiness with financial stability. Then when we could not attain it, we will say, 'Oh, I am a failure. I can never get things done the right way I wanted to.' Life-searching is not like that.

Life-searching is meant for us to be somewhat contended and contained in our everyday life. It is meant for us to be around people, for the people and with the people. It is not meant for us to be alone and aloof. Life-searching is a way of loving others too and loving ourselves more.

We need to have our own space in life. Thus we need too to give others the space to grow in love and care. By having the spaces in us and in others, we will gain dignity with openness. We need to have that space awareness to let others know that we care.

It means that we need to be ourselves, searching the very essence of life within us. We have life in us, having the ability to carry on to be affordable in living harmoniously with others around us, our friends, family members and the community. If we have obtained this kind of attitude, we have already reached the top in searching what we want.

More often than not, most of us go the wrong way to life-searching. We search the wrong things at the wrong time. We tend to be in the wrong place at the wrong time. We are never right in living a better life. We think we have searched all our life and that is enough to reach life stability.

This is not so, we need to continue search all through our whole life, till the day we have to say goodbye to Mother Earth. Our journey is not over yet. We can still search and search but are we satisfied? Life-searching means to have a fruitful life to live a comfortable life in terms of getting ourselves be more prepared for a better living environment. So are we still life-searching? Yes do carry on to search and search not to stop. We must try to achieve our goals to where we want to go and say 'hey' I have reached the climax and attain my achievement. Then I say you have completed your journey in life-searching.

> *"On a deeper level you are already complete. When you realize that, there is a playful joyous energy behind what you do." – Eckhart Tolle*

I feel what the words meant was what you are looking for, the only way is to find yourself to turn inwards. That is where you will find that were there all along.

The end result is what Antoine de Saint-Exupery quoted: *"Each man must look to himself to teach him the meaning of life. It is not something discovered: it is something moulded."*

Yet again there is another quotation from Joseph Campbell which said it all.

"Life is without meaning. You bring the meaning to it. The meaning of life is whatever you ascribe it to be. Being alive is the meaning."

Thus dear reader, it is in living that we can have life-searching. To search our own destiny of what we really desire and what we want to do in our life. It would be too late, if we do not begin in life-searching. Our life journey could end any time if we do not take stock of what we do during our lifetime.

Finally dear reader, do take care of yourself in living a more fruitful life on earth. It is about time we do reflections. What do we want out of our lives? What can we achieve on this earth so as to be contented and satisfied, being happy with people and our loved ones around.

References:

1. Abraham Lincoln (1809-1865)
2. Albert Camus
3. Albert Einstein
4. Anthony de Mello
5. Antoine de Saint-Exupery
6. Bradley Trevor Grieve
7. Confucius
8. Daisaku Ikeda
9. Dale Carnegie
10. Denis Waitley
11. Eckhart Tolle
12. Eddie Fisher (1954) – "Oh, My Papa"
13. Edwin Markham (1842-1940), Poet
14. George Bernard Shaw
15. Guatama Buddha

16. Howard Falco
17. Jim Rohn
18. Joel Osteen
19. John Powell, S.J
20. Joseph Campbell
21. Journey With Me –(http:/journey withme.info)
22. Mahatma Ghandi
23. Maria Robinson
24. Martin Luther King Jr.
25. Mike &The Mechanics – The Living Years
26. Mother Teresa
27. Neville Goddard (1905-1972)
28. Norman Vincent Peale
29. Oprah Winfrey
30. Richard Templar
31. Saint Bernard of Clairvox (1090-1153), Christian Monk & Mystic
32. Saint Francis of Assisi
33. Scott Dinsmore
34. Victor Frankl
35. William James

Printed in the United States
By Bookmasters